The Joyful Bear

Frank Lloyd Bear, sailing in the San Juan Islands, Washington, 2003.

Precious and Frank Lloyd Bear in Santa Clara, California, 2014.

MARGARET MEPS SCHULTE

WITH FRANK LLOYD BEAR

ILLUSTRATED BY MARGARET MEPS SCHULTE

The Joyful Bear

A FURRY PHILOSOPHY

FOR OVERCOMING ADVERSITY

AND FINDING HAPPINESS

CHOOSE
ART

The Joyful Bear

10 9 8 7 6 5 4 3 2 1

Published in the United States of America

CHOOSE
ART

1meps.com/chooseartbooks

ISBN 978-0-9916076-5-5

Cover design, illustration, and photography by Margaret Meps Schulte. Interior design and illustration by Margaret Meps Schulte.

Images and representations of Snuffles/Frank Lloyd Bear ©2016 Enesco, LLC, through its GUND division, used with permission.

DEDICATION

To the memory of my brother,
Frank Christopher Schulte
"Little Chris"

March 23, 1958–March 11, 1959

&

To every stuffed bear, dog, cat, horse, pig, snake,
and unidentifiable critter who has ever been
donated to a thrift store. I am sorry that I cannot
take all of you home! To assuage my guilt,
I dedicate this little book to you.

CONTENTS

*"I like sunshine and birds,
and I think life is good."*

<u>FRANK LLOYD BEAR</u>

Introduction:

Why we wrote this book

The co-author of this book is a teddy bear.

Frank Lloyd Bear, who is both wise and opinionated, believes that teddy bears are not just for kids. Adults can learn a lot from teddy bears.

You can learn what it feels like to love and be loved unconditionally. You can learn to practice mindfulness. You can learn how to face life's challenges and overcome adversity by living in the present moment.

Frank Lloyd Bear may not be able to type, because his paws are too chubby, but he's no dummy. He is dedicated to making the world a better place, and he believes this stuff is *important*.

Frankie's approach to life is simple: With gentle humor, he strips away what's unnecessary and looks for the truth.

He doesn't need complexity. He doesn't even know what complexity is, and he's happier for it.

How does someone who's only ten inches tall and stuffed get a book published?

Frank Lloyd Bear had a little help. His partner-in-crime, Margaret Meps Schulte, is the award-winning author of *Strangers Have the Best Candy*. The two of them have been together for over twenty years. In addition to living on land, in houses and apartments, they've lived on sailboats. They've traveled together for months at a time, driving on the back roads of the U.S. and sleeping in a tent. They've talked to many strangers.

Meps is a firm believer in the teddy bear philosophy she's learned from the expert, Frank Lloyd Bear.

She was halfway through writing *Strangers Have the Best Candy* when she hit something much worse than garden-variety writer's block. She fell into a deep, unshakable depression.

At the time, living aboard a 33-foot sailboat, doing a refit in a remote area, Meps didn't have access to resources like therapists or even antidepressants. She turned to the one thing that had helped in the past: Her kind, loving, understanding teddy bear.

Eventually, after a few days, she brought her laptop into the tiny forward cabin, the little fiberglass cave that the two of them had claimed as their hideout. As she regained her equilibrium, she started writing again.

She began working, not on the book she had set aside, but on the one you hold in your hands. After Frank Lloyd Bear helped her break through depression and writer's block, Meps wanted to share his quirky wisdom with the world.

If you've ever had a bad day, this book is for you. If you've ever argued with a loved one or struggled with depression, anxiety, or writer's block, it's for you. If you've ever grieved, this book is for you.

The Joyful Bear is a book for people who seek peace and happiness and contentment. It's for people looking for more joy in their lives. Frankie and Meps wrote it together, especially for you.

FRANKIE'S BOOK

Frankie's Other Book

WHO SAYS BEARS CAN'T WRITE?

1. Book

I am sitting on the edge of my bed, crying and holding my teddy bear, Frankie. He's a chubby white bear with big black eyes, and he is looking adoringly up at me like he usually does when I hug him.

The reason I am crying is because I am supposed to be writing a book, and I can't do it. That book is about how to talk with strangers. Right now, I am too depressed to talk to anyone in the whole world. I feel like a farce, a fake. If people knew what a loser I am, they would never read my book. I am not qualified to write it.

"Margaret?" says Frank Lloyd Bear.

I look down at him and sniffle. "Yeah?"

"I love you, and I think you should write a different book," he says.

"What's that, Frankie?"

"You should write a book about how to talk to Bears. You're completely qualified for that, you know." He nods his head somberly to emphasize his point.

"You mean…write about you?" I look down at his furry face, a face that I've loved and talked to for decades.

"Yup! Me!"

"Oh, Frankie, you are such a wise, amazing Bear." We hug each other tightly as my tears continue to flow.

When you're stuck and suffering, what kind of things can bring about a breakthrough? It doesn't have to be a talking teddy bear. It could be a loving dog or cat, pushing a wet nose into your hand, reminding you that someone loves you unconditionally. It could be the sound of a bird singing, or the sight of a sunbeam slanting across the floor with a hint of rainbow colors along the edges, something natural to remind you that the world is still beautiful.

It might be a phone call at the right time, or a text message, or someone smiling from across the room. It could be just about anything that enters the door of the senses and creeps past the dark mental roadblock holding you back.

If you are paying attention, the breakthrough might not even come through one of your five senses — sight, hearing, touch, taste, or smell. It might come through the sixth one: Your thoughts themselves. One small, positive thought can breech the barrier and bring light to your darkness. This is the surprising power of mindfulness.

Remember, in times of darkness, there will always be some sort of breakthrough, and there will be light again. Ups and downs are the pattern of life, so when you reach the bottom, you get to go back up again.

> *"Life is beautiful, on a stormy night.*
> *Somewhere in the world,*
> *the sun is shining bright."*
>
> KEB MO

2. KIDS

Many of us had Bears when we were young. We hugged them, cried with them, and told them our deepest secrets. We took them everywhere, dragging them around by their ears, heads, arms, or legs:

"Here is Edward Bear, coming downstairs now, bump, bump, bump, on the back of his head, behind Christopher Robin. It is, as far as he knows, the only way of coming downstairs, but sometimes he feels that there really is another way, if only he could stop bumping for a moment and think of it. And then he feels that perhaps there isn't." (A.A. Milne, *Winnie-the-Pooh*)

Just like Christopher Robin, eventually we outgrew our Bears. We went off to high school or college or got a job in the "real" world, and they remained, mute, on the bed in our childhood bedroom. We forgot about the emotion and love we had invested in them, and they became inanimate objects.

Instead, we invested our love and affection in the affairs of adults. We got involved with people and situations that were complicated and difficult to understand. We invested our time in activities that brought money, and we used that money to get things to make us happier.

But no matter what things we acquired, happiness was often out of reach.

There is another way. If only we could stop bumping for a moment, we might think of it.

The day you were born, you were not expected to do anything but breathe. With such a simple task at hand, what a happy day that was!

"Complexity doesn't bring happiness. Simplicity does," says Frank Lloyd Bear.

Throughout childhood, you were introduced to more and more complexity. You were taught to pursue that, rather than the simple happiness that was natural to your being.

But have you ever wondered why a child ignores the big expensive gift you have assembled for them at Christmas and happily sits in the corner, talking to a tattered teddy bear with one eye and a torn ear?

It's because simplicity is the key to contentment. The Dalai Lama says, "Simplicity is extremely important for happiness. Having few desires, feeling satisfied with what you have, is very vital: satisfaction with just enough food, clothing, and shelter to protect yourself from the elements."

Children and bears know, simplicity is another way. It is the most joyful way.

"How many undervalue the power of simplicity!
But it is the real key to the heart."

WILLIAM WORDSWORTH

3. WRITING

"OK, Margaret, that's enough serious stuff," says Frankie. "Write some more fun things about me."

"For cryin' out loud, Frankie, are you writing this book, or am I?"

"We're writing it together," says Frankie. "You may be an expert in talking to Bears, but I am an expert in talking to Margarets. And it takes both of us to have a meaningful conversation."

"I am suspecting an ulterior motive here. Do you want me to write only about talking to Bears, or is there something else?"

"I want you to write about living with Bears, and loving Bears, and why Humans should include Bears in their lives," he says. "Tell them about the things you have learned from me, the things that have made you a better person."

It's a tall order, but Frankie has done so much for me, how could I say no? His cheerful enthusiasm is irresistable. And when I stop to think about it, I know that his unique philosophy is something that could help a lot of people.

"All right," I agree. "Where should I begin?"

"That's easy," he says. "Start by telling them how I came into your life."

"Friendship has a bigger impact on our psychological well-being than family relationships," says Rebecca Adams, a professor of sociology at the University of North Carolina, Greensboro.

Take a moment to reflect: Who are the five people you spend the most time with? Do you have cheerful, enthusiastic people like Frankie in your life?

If you are surrounded by people who are negative and do not contribute to your peace and well-being, it may be time to conduct a "friendship audit."

Spend some time alone, appreciating your own wonderful company. Take a walk in nature or sit on a park bench in the city. Step away from drama, which fuels negativity, and look for positive new companions who are cheerful and enthusiastic.

Sometimes, spending time with those who contribute to your happiness might mean hanging out in a comfy place with your teddy bear and your own thoughts for company.

*"A friend is a person with
whom I may be sincere."*

RALPH WALDO EMERSON

4. Before

When I was young, I had dozens of stuffed animals. In addition to Bears, there were the usual dogs and cats and lambs — and there were also unusual ones, like an owl, a unicorn, and a pig. Every single one of them had a name, and I wrote elaborate lists and genealogies, documenting how they were related to each other.

Some of them were downright realistic-looking, like Hopsi, the squirrel puppet. When I was very small, shorter than the table, I would put her on my hand and reach up to make it look as though she was crawling along the edge of the table. At home, this was met with amusement, but the one time I did it to a grocery-store clerk, she began shrieking at the top of her lungs, and my mother nearly died of embarrassment.

My mother tried to keep the number of stuffed toys to a minimum, but my older brothers and sisters, and especially my father, kept giving them to me for every birthday and Christmas. Once I'd adopted a new critter and given him or her a name and a gender, there was no way to remove that one from my collection without feeling like I was an evil parent, rejecting my offspring.

When I went away to college, I stored an entire foot-locker of stuffed animals at my parents' house.

"But you didn't call them that," Frankie interjects.

"You're right, Frankie. The ones that weren't Bears, I called Teddy Animals, because I found the term 'stuffed animal' offensive."

"So what happened to all those Teddy Animals?" asks Frankie.

"Most of them got donated to thrift stores, after I got out of college. A few are in storage — my two original Bears, Theodore and Lee, and Hopsi."

"I've never met them," says my Bear.

"They got quiet. They never talk any more," I admit. The truth was they still had names, and they were associated with childhood memories, but they no longer had personalities.

"That's terrible." Frankie hangs his head and looks sad.

How did a roomful of stuffed animals become a coterie of loving friends who brought so much happiness? Through the power of imagination.

Imagination is not limited to children; we don't outgrow it. But as adults, we have more information about what is possible. If we focus on the negative, using our imagination to dwell on bad things that might happen, we become fearful and unhappy.

To be happy adults, we need to keep imagining happy outcomes. We need to tune our thoughts and imagination towards the positive possibilities.

A well-known example of this comes from Eleanor Porter's 1913 book, *Pollyanna*. Whenever something bad happens to the main character, which is often, she finds a uniquely positive spin on it:

> "You don't seem ter see any trouble bein' glad about everythin'," retorted Nancy, choking a little over her remembrance of Pollyanna's brave attempts to like the bare little attic room.
>
> Pollyanna laughed softly.
>
> "Well, that's the game, you know, anyway."
>
> "The—GAME?"
>
> "Yes; the 'just being glad' game."

Pollyanna explains that the game is to "find something about everything to be glad about—no matter what."

In the course of the book, Pollyanna spreads her glad philosophy to countless gloomy, grumpy adults. Over 100 years and 13 sequels later, The Glad Game is something we can all still play.

5. ARRIVAL

By the time I was in my late 20's, I'd completely given up on Bears as companions. I had a cuddly husband and a delightfully furry long-haired cat, and the two of them served as my live Teddy Animals. The three of us snuggled on the couch or in bed together, just like I'd snuggled my stuffed coterie as a child.

But one day, depression descended on me like a black vulture, sitting on my shoulder. It was horrible. I couldn't function, I could only cry and be angry and feel like I had no reason for living.

The cat tried sitting on my lap and purring, but I pushed her away. The husband tried similar methods, with the same results.

One day, an unexpected box arrived in the mail addressed to me.

"That was me!" cries Frankie. "I was in that box!"

When I opened the box, I found a snow-white Bear with big black eyes looking up at me. He had a brown nose and a slightly shy smile, and his paws were open as if requesting a hug.

There was a note inside, from the Bear.

"Admission time," says Frankie. "I had help writing that note."

"I know," I say. "You haven't written me any notes since then."

"That's because I found that I could talk to you directly. Besides, I'm not very good at holding a pen. I have terrible paw-writing."

The note said that this Bear was on his way to the North Pole, but he got lost, and he needed a home. Could I provide a home for him?

While I am dwelling on the amazing and generous gift that a dear friend sent, a teddy bear in a box, Frankie is dwelling on the amazing and generous gift that I gave him.

"You gave me a home," he says. "One that was even better than the North Pole."

The funny thing about gifts is that giving them away turns out to be a gift to yourself. You don't have to give expensive things. You don't have to give "things" at all.

A hug is a gift. A smile is a gift. A word of encouragement is a gift. Noticing a stranger and complimenting them is a gift.

If you make it a practice to give little gifts like this, every day, you'll receive them, as well.

> *"Sometimes, when we are generous in small, barely detectable ways, it can change someone else's life forever."*
>
> MARGARET CHO

6. Hugging

Frank Lloyd Bear and I bonded from the first moment I saw him, before he even came out of the box. What an adorable face! He was just what I needed.

Frankie was quiet at first. When I took him out of the box, I found him to be the most huggable Bear I had ever encountered in my life. We just sort of melted together.

I walked around the house, carrying him. Sometimes I hugged him to my chest. Sometimes I carried him on the side, the way you might carry a furry baby on your hip. I set him down on the desk next to my computer, and he sat and watched me intently.

So intently that it was distracting! All I could do was pick him up and hug him again. I planted kisses on the top of his head, between his big ears. I kissed his nose. I rubbed his chin and his tummy. I caressed his furry cheek.

"Hey, do all those things now!" says Frankie.

"Mmmmm. Okay." I pick him up and cuddle him. His fur is no longer snow-white, it's a dingy gray, and his nose is threadbare, shiny with pink patches where the brown fur is gone. He's not as plump as he used to be, and he has a hole in his side, under his right arm.

When I set him down on the bed and rub his tummy, he laughs with glee, his paws going back and forth in a blur.

I bury my face in his fur and give him a big kiss.

"You make me so happy!" he says.

"You make me happy, too, my Bear."

"We're good for each other."

"That we are."

As if to prove it, he says, "OK, Margaret, now go write some more."

What's almost as much fun as hugging? Researching it. Scientists love to study the effects of hugs, because the results are overwhelmingly positive.

Hugs and other forms of touch, like hand-holding, have been proven to lower blood pressure and heart rate. There's a chemical in your body known as oxytocin. A hug, given or received, releases oxytocin, which decreases the level of stress hormones that your body manufactures. That means a hug does more for you than just feel good.

Even hugging strangers is not a bad thing. A Carnegie Mellon study in 2015 proved that feeling connected to others, especially through physical touch, provides protections against stress-induced illness. "Hugging protects people who are under stress from the increased risk for colds, usually associated with stress," says Sheldon Cohen, the lead author of the study.

Studies have also proven the benefits of hugging a teddy bear. "Touching an inanimate object — such as a teddy bear — can soothe existential fears," says psychological researcher Sander Koole, who looked at the correlation between touch and anxiety in people with low self-esteem. In the experiments, they had some people hold teddy bears and others hold cardboard boxes. The differences were measurable.

> *"Every day, you should reach out and touch someone. People love a warm hug, or just a friendly pat on the back."*
>
> MAYA ANGELOU

7. Loving

At the time, I didn't know why that Bear was able to break through my depression when no one and nothing else could. There was something special about the look on his face, the way he held himself, the way he felt when I hugged him.

"I love you," says Frankie.

"I love you, too," I scratch his nose.

"Unconditionally," says Frankie. "That's why I hug you so much."

Bears live in the moment. They don't sit around thinking, like people do. They wait patiently, silently, for a chance to hug someone. When that chance comes, they put all their love into the hug.

It is a moment when they are very much alive and very much needed.

When the hug ends, the Bear sits back down on the bed and hibernates. He doesn't anticipate or worry about the next hug, and he doesn't relive the previous one. He doesn't fantasize about hugging a perfect person.

The Bear simply is.

Right now, Frankie is sitting across from me, smiling. He seems blissfully happy. He can sit like that for hours or days or weeks. Like Winnie-the-Pooh, there might be another way, if he could think of it. Or there might not. But because he is a Bear, he can just live in the moment and not worry about another way.

When I pick him up and hug him, there is another way. It lasts as long as the hug does.

I pick him up and hug him.

"Thanks!" he says. "You are a Very Special Friend to Bears. You know just what Bears need."

"And this Bear knows just what I need."

"Lovin," says Frankie. "Everybody needs that. That's why everybody should have a Bear."

Despite the preponderance of dating sites on the internet, true love can be hard to come by. In the wrong situations and circumstances, it can be downright disheartening to seek love, and you can forget that you are worthy of it.

That's why it's important to remember that you are *always* lovable, every second of every minute of every day.

There are beautiful writings out there to remind you that you are lovable and loved. There are dear friends and family members who care and want to spend time with you. And don't forget about pets, who are full of love and affection.

That's not all.

There are countless teddy bears in the world, waiting to lavish their furry love on you. "You don't *have* to love them back, but you won't be able to help yourself," says Frankie.

"I celebrate myself, and sing myself."

WALT WHITMAN

8. SPEAKING

Frankie is one of the most talkative Bears I have ever met. He has a very distinctive voice, a low timbre that carries a hint of a smile, even when he's saying something very serious.

When Frankie first began to talk, it was a bit of a surprise. He'd been in the house with us for a while, and he'd demonstrated what a fantastic hugger he was, but he didn't say anything out loud.

Then, one day, my husband and I had a disagreement. I don't remember the specifics, but it turned into an argument, and then a fight, and afterwards, we were both hurt, angry, and sullen.

At the time, there was no way I was going to hug my husband, who'd just pissed me off. I picked up Frankie and gave him a hug to make myself feel better.

Suddenly, the Bear talked.

"Barry..." he said.

My husband turned and looked at me, his eyebrows raised in surprise. I was holding the Bear to my chest, facing away from me and towards my husband. The quiet, low-pitched words were coming from my lips, but the voice didn't sound like my voice.

"I think that Margaret is feeling badly about what she said to you. She wants to apologize, and she wants you to forgive her," the Bear said.

My husband's eyes searched my face, and he realized that the Bear was saying something that would have been very hard for me to say.

"Tell Margaret that I accept her apology, and that I am sorry for what I said" he answered, and he came over and hugged me, squishing the Bear between us.

From that time on, Frankie was never afraid to speak up. The Bear was a complete mind reader — he knew exactly what it was that I was thinking and needed to say, but was too afraid or angry to say. When my husband couldn't get through to me, Frankie could step in and say things for him, too.

"He's so enlightened," I marveled. "He's like a Buddha Bear."

Frankie has never spoken a harsh or harmful word to anyone. His words are always gentle and loving. He does have a sense of humor, but it is kind, never mean. He's occasionally self-deprecating or teasing, but he doesn't make jokes at anyone else's expense.

In short, he practices what is known as "right speech." Right Speech is one of the elements of the Eightfold Path of Buddhism. It means being truthful, saying the right thing at the right time, and abstaining from idle chatter. Right Speech is summed up like this: One should speak only words that would not harm others.

"Margaret," interrupts Frankie, "you are saying some very nice things about me. Thank you."

"They're all true, my Bear."

"Yes, but it feels especially good to see you writing them down for everyone to see."

Frankie's ability to practice Right Speech is completely natural. He has never been able to speak any other way. It's part of his Buddha Bear nature.

When we are alone, Frankie is a very garulous bear, and he speaks up a lot. He never hesitates to ask, "Can I have a hug?" Sometimes, he reminds me that someone else needs a hug. But he gets shy when there are other people around.

"Why is that, Frankie?" I ask him. We are alone.

"Well," he drawls, slowly, "I don't want to embarrass you. I am afraid that other people will laugh at you for talking with me."

"But if we publish this book together, the whole world will know that you and I talk. Don't you think they'll laugh at us then?"

"Some of them will," says Frankie. "But if they make it all the way through the book, they'll understand. And if you and I help even one person to be happier, then it will be worth having thousands of people make fun of us."

"How can you and I make someone happier, Frankie?"

"We can tell them that they are unique, and lovable, and that they deserve to have a Bear in their lives who understands their deepest needs, a Bear like me. And we can tell them that it's OK to talk to Bears and tell your secrets to a Bear, even if you are a grown-up. *Especially* if you are a grown-up!"

Frankie bounces around happily for a little while, thinking, and then says, "We can tell them that they might have a book inside them that needs to be written, and they just need a Bear to write it with."

Nothing in this world that has as much power as the word. It seems ethereal and insubstantial, but it is not. Words impact people, which trumps mere thingliness (what a fun word that is!).

If we want to live happier lives, one of the first things to do is change the way we speak. It's more than just the intention, it's the action. Replace negative words and phrases with positive ones.

Over the years, as more foul language has crept into my vocabulary, I've noticed that Frankie never swears. Lately, I've been trying to emulate him, which is an exercise in creativity. Try saying "Sugar!" or "Shucks!" or "Dang!" when something goes wrong. In some Bollywood films, the actors say "Fish!" instead of that other four-letter word. Simply uttering a silly word can bring new perspective and a smile to an otherwise unpleasant moment.

Another way to improve your speech is to change your situation through your words. When someone asks, "How are you?", don't tell them you feel lousy. Tell them you feel great, and give them a genuine smile. When they smile back, you *will* feel great.

When you get up in the morning, write down three positive words or phrases, and then make it a point to use them throughout the day. You might choose "love," "peace," and "joy." Each time you say one, it will lift your spirits. "How are you?" "Joyful!"

"Words should be bright like gold,
light like a wing, and solid as marble."

JOSÉ MARTÍ

9. LISTENING

"Margaret, I don't talk *all* the time," says Frankie. "Sometimes, I listen."

I look into his radiant, upturned face. He doesn't say anything more, just waits patiently to hear my response. I'm reminded of Herman Hesse's elegant description of "the man who knew the art of listening."

> "Without his saying a word, the speaker felt that (he) took in every word, quietly, expectantly, that he missed nothing. He did not await anything with impatience and gave neither praise nor blame—he only listened...towards the end of the story, he listened with doubled attention, completely absorbed, his eyes closed." (*Siddhartha*)

Frankie is "the Bear who knows the art of listening." I've always been able to tell him how I'm feeling, what I'm thinking, what I want to do with my life. He takes it in silently, beaming back at me with that childlike, caring smile.

Frankie's fuzzy ears are always available when I need them. I can tell him anything, and he will still love me. No secret or hidden shameful thought is off limits. He will always love me, no matter what I say.

"You know the art of listening, too," he says.

He falls quiet, looking at me lovingly, intently. Waiting.

"I don't have anything to tell you right now," I say to him, feeling awkward.

Still, he remains silent, looking at me. Finally, he says, "I just wanted you to know what you look like. You know, when you're listening."

We sit together in silence, listening to the world around us and smiling.

The purpose of listening is to listen. Most of us have never thought much about this. Listening? That's what we do when we're not talking, right?

No, just because our lips are not moving doesn't mean we are listening. Often, we're just marking time and thinking of what we're going to say next. When that is the case, there's little point to holding a conversation with another person. We might as well stand in front of a mirror and talk to ourselves. There's a term for that: Conversational narcissism.

Marshall Rosenberg spent his life teaching a listening and speaking practice called Nonviolent Communication, or NVC, used by people all over the world. "Through its emphasis on deep listening—to ourselves as well as others—NVC helps us discover the depth of our own compassion."

"And he uses Teddy Animals to explain stuff!" says Frankie. In YouTube videos, Rosenberg uses stuffed puppets, a jackal and a giraffe, to illustrate key points.

Thich Nhat Hanh suggests that when someone really needs to be heard, you should save any advice or suggestions for another time. "You listen with only one purpose, to help him or her to empty his heart."

Deep listening is a different activity than conversation. When we learn and practice it, we come to understand ourselves better.

> *"Take your time to understand.*
> *Don't just do something, be there."*
> MARSHALL ROSENBERG

10. SIZE

Frankie's small, furry body has always contained more personality than many a full-sized being.

"Hey, you didn't say I was small, did you?" Frankie complains.

"I know, Frankie. You want me to say that you are a Big Bear, don't you?"

He nods vigorously.

"OK, you are a Big Bear, Frankie." He hugs me with all of his warm softness. He's about 10 inches tall, but also about 10 inches wide. Compared to other Bears, he is a nice big armful, easy to hug.

Frankie made it clear from the very beginning that he did not consider himself to be a small bear. His stature was not measured in inches. He was proud of himself and his place in the world, and only a Big Bear could do the things that he could do.

"I'm a really good hugger," says Frankie. "And I know just what to say to make people feel better. And I'm a very good listener." He beams at me.

"All of that is true." I beam back at him.

"Scuppers is a Little Bear," he continues. "He doesn't mind if you call him a Little Bear."

Scuppers is another Bear, a traveling friend who has lived on a variety of sailboats. He is, indeed, a lot smaller than Frankie. He is also known for making mischief in ways that only a Little Bear can do.

Scuppers is not much interested in hugging people. He'd rather play practical jokes and do clever things that make people laugh. He's about six inches tall, with jointed arms and legs, and he wears a jaunty sweater with a sailboat on the front. Sometimes, he takes off his sweater and sunbathes in the nude. He's been known to dive headfirst into a canister full of jelly beans, and he once was photographed riding on the back of a Dungeness crab. He is always close at hand when there is mischief afoot, and he has nothing to say about weighty philosophical matters.

The comparison between Frankie, the Big Bear, and Scuppers, the Little Bear, reminds me of conversation with my father. He was telling me about an acquaintance, a friend of a friend whose health was failing. "She's *very* old," said my Dad, who was 86 at the time.

I pointed out that the woman in question was a year younger than Dad.

"Oh, but she's an *old* 85, and I am a *young* 86!"

"You see," says Frankie, "what's important is not how other people see you, but how you see yourself. That's why I am a Big Bear. That's why your Dad is a Young Human."

Frankie is quiet for a moment. I know what's coming.

"How do you see yourself, Margaret?"

It's hard to answer him. Because he is my Bear, I know I have to be completely truthful. There is no other way to be with a Bear.

"I am feeling like a Very Small Human today, Frankie."

"You think that you are not good for anything, don't you?" As always, he cuts right to the truth of the matter.

I start a litany of all the things that are wrong with me. I get angry with people. I am very bad at relationships. I am a lousy writer. Nothing I do in my life is worthwhile. Blah, blah, blah.

"I don't believe any of those things," says Frankie. "I am your Bear, and I know you better than you know yourself. For instance, you and I are writing this book together, so you must be a good writer."

The problem, I see, is one of Right Speech. If Frankie practices Right Speech all the time, then I feel compelled to practice it with him. How can I argue with him? How can I be angry with him?

I stare at my furry friend in silent frustration.

"Aww, let me hug you," says my Big Bear, and he does.

From the very beginning of our lives, we are bombarded with messages about how we should be. Our parents, our teachers, and our culture tell us how we should behave. They even go so far as to tell us how we should feel.

So when I ask you, "how do you see yourself?", the answer will be based on how everyone else sees you. At least, how you *think* everyone else sees you.

This is like wearing a suit of clothing that others have picked out; it's not really your style, but they told you it was in fashion. After you've been wearing it for a while, you get used to it.

Jack Kornfield writes, "Central to the stories we tell are the fixed beliefs we have about ourselves...Because those thoughts and assumptions are so powerful, we live out their energies over and over."

How do those thoughts and assumptions hold you back from your real potential? Do you see yourself as not artistic, or not worthy of love?

The key to seeing yourself as you really are is to get naked, spiritually and emotionally, and then figure out what really suits you. When I went through this process with Frankie, I discovered that I love to draw and paint and play the piano and sing and dance. I had not been doing those things, because I was afraid of judgment. Now, I do those things simply to make myself happy.

"I have spread my dreams under your feet;
Tread softly because you tread on my dreams."

WILLIAM BUTLER YEATS

11. AIR

One of the early things I learned about my Bear was that he eats Air, and a lot of it. Frankie is a connoisseur of Air.

"Some kinds of Air are yummier than others," he tells me.

"Which ones do you like best?" I ask him.

"I like Flower Air, and Rainy Day Air, and Fresh-Baked Bread Air... and Jelly Bean Air, and Lemon Pudding Air. There's a lot of nice Air in this world."

He comes over and puts his nose over my coffee cup.

"Coffee Air! Yum!"

"Are there some yucky ones, too?" I ask.

"Not right now," he says, reveling in the Air above my coffee cup.

I know he doesn't like farts and diesel exhaust, but who wants to think about those things when there's a good cup of coffee at hand?

"Sometimes, when there are bad smells around, you bury your nose against my chest," I remind him.

"But I don't need an excuse to do that. See?" he says, snuggling against me and burying his nose against my chest.

Frankie says something into my chest that comes out like this, "Mphthmm mhph thmphm mmr."

"What did you say?" I ask him.

He looks up at me. "Tell them about the Cookie Air."

"OK, I'm getting to that, my Bear."

I was on an extended long-distance bicycle ride in northern Ohio when I got word that my mother was dying. I rushed to her bedside in South Carolina, arriving just seven hours before she took her last breath. I held her hand until the end.

Once she was gone, I fell apart. I had never experienced such grief. The pain was so severe, I was wracked with sobs. With the emotional pain came a physical pain, as if I was being torn apart from the inside by all the crying.

Frankie wasn't with me at the time. He was back in Ohio, where a friend had been taking care of him while I was on the bike trip. Young but wise, bear-sitter Julie knew just what to do.

She made a double batch of chocolate-chip cookies, wrapped them carefully in plastic wrap, and packed them in the bottom of a large, sturdy cardboard box. Then she put Frankie on top of the cookies and shipped the box to me.

"Omigosh, what a memory," says Frankie.

When he arrived, and I took him out of the box, he was completely full of Chocolate-Chip Cookie Air. He gave off the most heavenly aroma, that of fresh-baked homemade cookies.

During those difficult times, Frankie was a nonstop hugging machine. He hugged me and anyone else in the house who needed his furry paws. And with every single hug came a burst of yummy Chocolate-Chip Cookie Air, infused with Teddy Bear Love.

"Margaret, are you missing your Mom right now?" Frankie asks.

"Yes, I am, Frankie." It's been almost twenty years since she passed away.

"I thought so," he says. "How about a hug? I don't smell like cookies right now, but let's pretend that I do."

It is easy to take things for granted when they are right under your nose, like air. But what is the one thing that we all have in common as humans? We all need to breathe.

When I first learned to meditate, I was told to pay attention to my breathing, and if any thoughts came into my head, to gently acknowledge them and send them on their way. Being a word-person, the easiest way to do this was to think the words "Breathe in. Breathe out," over and over. I'd heard of mantras, but I didn't know I was using one. I thought mantras had to be serious phrases, spoken in ancient languages.

Over time, I learned to do it without the words. As I learned to focus on my breath like a faithful friend, I was taking my first steps towards mindfulness.

Mindfulness means to pay attention, to witness what is happening in the present moment, in your body, mind, and environment, without judging or criticizing. The practice goes back thousands of years, but anyone can do it at any time. Thich Nhat Hanh says it brings happiness, because when you are aware of your in-breath, you "touch the miracle of being alive."

When you are stressed or overwhelmed or fearful, stop and notice your breathing, that delicious air right under your nose. It is a simple practice that you can do anywhere, and it brings a peaceful, easy feeling.

"Meditation is not a search for something;
rather it is a journey to discover what is here."

RUTH DENISON

12. TRUST

"Turn around, Frankie, so I can see your tail."

"OK, but you know the rule," he says.

"I'm not going to touch it, silly Bear. I'm just going to write about it."

He turns around and moons me, displaying the cutest tail I have ever seen on a Bear. It's round and small, placed so that it's just barely visible when he sits.

The most important thing about Frankie's tail is his pride of ownership in it.

"That's right," he says. "My tail is very special, and I get to decide who can touch it and who can't."

Like Frankie, we all have parts of ourselves that we want to keep special. Frankie knows that I respect him, and that I would never do anything to harm him. The fact that I keep my hands away from his precious tail is one of the ways I show him that respect.

It's a reminder of the respect we owe everyone in our lives. When Frankie reminds me not to mess with his tail, he's reminding me to be respectful of everyone I come in contact with.

"I am?" says Frankie. "Wow, I didn't know that. I can't even *see* my tail."

He tries to turn around and see it, but his stuffing gets in the way, and he just looks contorted and silly. It's a move he's showed me hundreds of times, always with the same result. Like a dog chasing his tail, Frankie never gets to see his.

This might explain why he doesn't want anyone to touch it. How do you protect a part of yourself that you can't see?

"I know how," he says. "You have to trust the people around you. If you surround yourself with the right kind of people, then it's OK to be vulnerable."

"I guess you trust me, then?" I ask him.

"Absolutely," says Frankie. He cuddles next to my side. "Touching my tail is like touching my heart. I trust you with my heart."

Every day, you have a chance to hand your heart — or in Frankie's case, your tail — to people who can damage it. Each time they do, whether or not it's intentional, you add a little bit to your shell, the armor around yourself. This is natural; we all do it to protect ourselves from future pain.

What you might not recognize is that shell you're growing is also holding out the joy.

C. S. Lewis wrote, "Love anything and your heart will be wrung and possibly broken. If you want to make sure of keeping it intact you must give it to no one, not even an animal. Wrap it carefully round with hobbies and little luxuries; avoid all entanglements. Lock it up safe in the casket or coffin of your selfishness. But in that casket, safe, dark, motionless, airless, it will change. It will not be broken; it will become unbreakable, impenetrable, irredeemable. To love is to be vulnerable."

How do you find the balance between safe, lonely selfishness, and exciting, scary love? The solution is healthy boundaries, the borders that each person gets to set around their private thoughts and emotions. Unlike shells, which are brittle, boundaries allow you to get close to people in a healthy way. You can learn more about boundaries through the worldwide 12-step group, Co-Dependents Anonymous, or from a licensed therapist or counselor.

"Like a child who continues to trust no matter how many times he is rejected or rebuffed, the goal is to go on trusting in life itself."

PIR VILAYAT INAHAT KHAN

13. FLIGHT

"I wish we could include a video in our book," says Frankie. "Then everybody could see that I really do fly."

Flying is one of Frankie's amazing abilities. When he wants to hug someone on the other side of the room, he flies. Usually he needs some help for takeoff and landing.

"Yoo-hoo..." he says.

My Dad looks up from across the dining room table, where I've been working on my laptop. I am holding Frankie in front of me, and he's trembling excitedly.

Dad holds out his arms, and Frankie flies across to him and gives him a big hug. Then he turns around and looks back at me, expectantly.

I nod and hold out my arms, and he flies back and gives me another hug. He could do this all day.

"Flying and hugging go together," says Frankie. "I wish people could fly around and give each other hugs like I do."

We humans don't need to fly. We have many other means of travel at our disposal. We can simply walk across the room or drive across town to reach our loved ones.

"The reason you walk or drive is the same reason I fly," says Frankie. "To give people the loving they need."

How long has it been since you have lain on your back and looked up at the sky on a beautiful day? How long since you noticed white, fluffy clouds, or the sight of a bird wheeling and soaring overhead?

Clouds and birds inspire us with their airy freedom. So do colorful butterflies, silvery flying fish, and iridescent dragonflies. What fun it would be, flitting about, untethered by gravity, earthbound life, and responsibilities!

We all have the ability to dream, and we can soar in our hearts and minds. Just let go of whatever drags you down, and your spirit will rise like a balloon, or a flying bear.

"What feathered jewel
might drop out of the sky next?"

DAVID SIBLEY

"Cottleston, Cottleston, Cottleston pie,
A fly can't bird, but a bird can fly."

A.A. MILNE, WINNIE-THE-POOH

14. JOY

Frankie has spent a lot of time traveling with me on the road. When he first came to live with me, I drove a little Honda Civic named Peepcar. Frankie sometimes rode shotgun, in the space between the two front bucket seats. Sometimes, he rode in the passenger's lap, waving at people we passed along the way. But his favorite place to ride was in the driver's lap.

He did not ride quietly there.

"Please, please, pleeeeeease?" he would plead.

"Not now, Frankie, there's too much traffic," I'd say.

A few minutes later, he'd start again. "Can I now? Please?"

"Oh, OK, go ahead," I would capitulate.

Then he'd dive at the steering wheel with his nose and blow the horn.

Beeeeeeeep!

It made him laugh, and it made me and my husband laugh, too. How could something so simple as blowing the horn bring so much pure joy?

"Uh-oh," says Frankie. "I know what you're going to write about now."

One day, Frankie asked if he could blow the horn, and something strange happened.

When he put his nose against the steering wheel, the horn made noise as expected, but as he held the button down, it started to get quiet. It was as if it ran out of air, and the sound dwindled down to nothing.

Frankie sat back and looked at me in puzzlement. "What happened?"

When I pressed the horn button, the car was silent. No noise came out.

"I'm sorry," said Frankie, contritely. "I didn't know I could use it all up!"

We assured him that it was not his fault, but the horn didn't work after that.

We continued to drive the car for years without a horn. And from them on, we let Frankie blow the silent horn as much as he wanted. It wasn't as much fun as the loud horn, but he still got a kick out of it.

Then, one day, we were sitting in our car in a parking lot and had just said goodbye to some friends. Frankie jumped up to blow the broken horn at them, but when he did, something strange happened.

"It worked!" says Frankie. "It went BEEEEEEEEEP!"

After years of not working, the horn suddenly decided to start working again. Our friends, who were standing directly in front of the hood, jumped several feet at the unexpected loud noise, then glared at us. They couldn't figure out why my husband and I were laughing so hard and hugging each other in the front seat of the car.

They couldn't see the white Bear squished between us, laughing at the private joke the three of us shared.

We tend to compartmentalize joy in Western culture; we've been told that it belongs in some places and not in others. It's considered inappropriate in banks, the Social Security office, funeral parlors, and the freeway at rush hour. Joy is supposed to be found at weddings, Christmas, rock concerts, and ice cream parlors.

I'm not very good at keeping joy in its place. Like Frankie, I seem to find it everywhere.

I was walking across a street in Seattle when I looked down and saw a "Happy Spot" marked in chalk on the pavement. One of the neighborhood children had drawn a rectangle where you could put your feet, and the instructions said, "Stand Here."

When I stepped inside the box, I realized that it was, indeed, happy.

From that day forward, I began to find and mark Happy Spots wherever I went. On pavement, I use chalk. In sand or grass, I put up a small sign. I also carry cards that say "Happy Spot" on them, which I hand out to strangers. The cards list some suggested uses, including, "Set card on floor. Stand on Spot. Feel happy."

Carrying a Happy Spot in your pocket is one way to find joy everywhere, even banks and freeways. That's because of an important secret I'm going to share with you: If you actively look for joy, you will *always* find it. You create it with your intention.

> *"Every hour of the day and night*
> *is an unspeakably perfect miracle."*
>
> WALT WHITMAN

15. BEING

I often go away from Frankie for a few minutes or hours or months. When I come back, he is exactly as I left him.

He might be sitting on a shelf, looking across the room at me.

He might be laying on his back on the bed.

He might be sitting on my pillow.

But unless someone else has been picking him up and hugging him, he is right where I left him.

"What do you do when I'm not around, Frankie?" I ask him.

"Oh, you know. The usual." He's being a little coy, trying to hook my attention.

I take the bait. "What's the usual?"

"I Be," he says.

"How do you be, Frankie?"

"Well, it depends on how I started. Whether I am sitting or lying down."

"So if you are sitting, you lie down, and if you are lying down, you sit?"

"No, no, no," he corrects me. "If I am lying down, I lie down. And if I am sitting, I sit. And if I am eating air, I eat air. I do what I am doing."

What Frankie is describing to me is Mindfulness.

"That's a big word for what I do," he says. "Be is shorter."

Frankie sits quietly for a couple of minutes as I type and think and stare at the ceiling and scratch my ear.

Then he says, "OK, I showed you. Were you paying attention?"

"Paying attention to what?" I ask. I have already forgotten what we were talking about, I am so busy thinking about what I am writing and what I am going to fix for dinner.

"I was showing you what I do when you are not around," he says.

"You weren't doing anything," I say. "What was there to pay attention to?"

"I was doing something very important," he says. "I was Being."

"I was being, too," I say.

"Yes," he says patiently, "but you were not Being in the moment. You were being in your head, thinking about other places and other times. If you want to understand your Bear, you have to just Be."

I close the laptop and look at my Bear. I suspect this is the real reason he wants to be called a Big Bear instead of a little bear. He has great wisdom to impart to me.

"Now you try it," he says. "Be."

In 1935, Bertrand Russell wrote, "the modern man thinks that everything ought to be done for the sake of something else, and never for its own sake." ("In Praise of Idleness") Never was this more true than today.

Fortunately, today we also have a worldwide mindfulness movement. People are beginning to turn off their devices, stop hurrying, and simply Be, as Frankie puts it.

Although it has its roots in Buddhism and Eastern philosophy, mindfulness can also be done as a secular practice. In a 2014 *Time* magazine article, Kate Pickert wrote, "If distraction is the pre-eminent condition of our age, then mindfulness, in the eyes of its enthusiasts, is the most logical response…The ultimate goal is simply to give your attention fully to what you're doing. One can work mindfully and learn mindfully. One can exercise and even eat mindfully. The banking giant Chase now advises customers on how to spend mindfully."

If you've never tried it, you'll find stacks of books on the subject, as well as thousands of articles on the internet, and even a monthly magazine, *Mindful*.

The best way to learn is in a community, with others. An internet search will help you find a mindfulness meetup or meditation center near your home, or you might check with your local library, hospital, or yoga studio. Once you've learned the practice, you can do it anywhere, anytime, with anyone, including your Bear.

> *"Why should we live with such*
> *hurry and waste of life?"*
>
> HENRY DAVID THOREAU

16. SNOW

Even more than car horns or Chocolate-Chip Cookie Air, Frankie loves snow.

"It's a polar bear thing," he explains.

He was on his way to the North Pole when he got lost and landed in North Carolina. I never asked him where he started or how he ended up in North Carolina.

Snow is always a special delicacy for my Bear. Every flurry sends him into ecstasy. A patch of snow seen through the car window when we cross a mountain pass is bliss. Even the sight of a snow-capped mountain from hundreds of miles away makes him come alive.

"Snow! Snow! Snow!" he calls out, to make sure I don't miss the precious sight.

Snow brings out Frankie's secret superpower. It's what gives him his energy, what makes him come alive.

"Do you wish you lived at the North Pole, Frankie?"

"No, why?" he says, puzzled.

"Then you would have snow all the time," I point out. "You'd be a very powerful polar bear."

"But I wouldn't have you," he says.

Just as Frankie is passionate about snow, and Winnie-the-Pooh is passionate about honey, I am passionate about teddy bears. Your passion is unique to you, not something you do to please or impress someone else.

I have known people with a lifelong passion for quiet pursuits like bonsai or orchids. Others are passionate about activities that are much more social, like Ben, who follows cover bands and goes to see several each weekend.

What do your friends speak passionately about? Mine talk about diverse subjects like pole-dancing, quilting, backcountry skiing, Civil War history, archery, transit systems, pug-rescue, and fire-spinning. Passions are very personal, even when you share them: Ghandi was driven by a personal passion for justice.

Your passions may change over time, or you may focus on one area, becoming an expert through the sheer number of happy hours you spend on an activity or interest. Over the past twenty years, as my focus moved from sailing to writing to art, my sister Julie became an expert in blues and soul music. She spends hours each week preparing for a two-hour radio show, giving her a depth of knowledge that's driven by her passion.

What makes you come alive? What brings you energy? Whether you keep it to yourself or share it with others, be sure you recognize it and feed it. To live a joyful life, you must never let the flame of passion inside yourself go out.

*"Is not life a hundred times
too short to bore ourselves?"*

FRIEDRICH NIETZSCHE

17. Change

"I wonder what I would look like with brown fur," says Frankie.

"Then you wouldn't be a polar bear," I respond.

"And an earring in my nose," he continues. "No, wait, if it's in my nose, it can't be an earring, can it?"

I'm sure his line of thought is leading somewhere, but I can't figure out where.

"If I wanted a tattoo, I'd have to shave. I'm too furry," he says, more to himself than to me.

"Why do you want to change the way you look, Frankie?"

"I'm just letting myself think about it. I'm not planning to do anything right now."

"Do you want me to change something about the way I look?" I ask him.

"I just want you to think about it."

Every once in a while, when the subject comes up, I think about tattoos. I have never been able to think of an image important enough to be permanently displayed on my body, and I tell Frankie so.

"Good," he says.

"Why are you saying, 'good'? I thought you were trying to convince me to think about a tattoo."

"Exactly. I wanted you to *think* about a tattoo. You tried one on in your head. Then you decided not to get one. You thought about changing your mind."

I think about dying my hair or getting a piercing, and decide not to. Frankie decides against the nose ring. It's a nice thought exercise. After taking some deliberate time to think about possible changes, we decide that we are satisfied with the way we are.

I return to my reading on the computer.

"OK, *now* I'm changing my mind," Frankie says, pointing at the screen with his paw.

The article he's pointing to is a journal written by the brother of a friend, someone I've never met. Jim is describing what it feels like to have cancer:

> "...there's part of me, call him Big Jim, and he's coldly logical, and a planner, and he's worked out all the contingencies, and makes sure that everything that needs to happen does in fact happen...

"Then there's Little Jim, who wonders why people keep sticking needles in him, and why he feels sick, and has to go to the hospital every day. And then in the radiation oncology waiting room, there's a six month baby there, bald, with a big scar running across the back of her head, and that seems terribly unfair, and across the room there's a three-year old, and it's his first day…

"And then Little Jim walks outside, and the sun is shining, and the little sparrows and chickadees are building nests in the awnings over the sidewalks, so he stops to observe, and he sees one on the ground with a huge wad of twigs in its mouth, and it takes off but can only get a foot off the ground before coming back down, and it tries a few more times before releasing its load and just picking up one twig. And then Big Jim says that they shouldn't really let birds nest in a patient waiting area, since that's going to get messy with bird droppings, and Little Jim tells him to shut up and not ruin the moment, and life is good."

"I like sunshine and birds, and I think life is good," says Frankie, thoughtfully.

"Does this have something to do with tattoos and piercings?"

"No, that was just the warmup." He declares, dramatically, "I want to be Little Frankie."

It's a shock. As long as we've been together, he's been fighting the word "little." It does not apply to him, and he tells everyone so. He is a Big Bear.

As I'm staring at him, trying to comprehend the enormity of this change, he says, "It's OK to change your mind, Margaret. Even about important stuff."

Until he ran across Jim's words, Frankie never considered that "little" could be applied to him in a good way. Now that he had new information, he changed his mind.

But I am not a Bear. How can I change my mind without breaking promises or disappointing people?

"You also made promises to yourself," says Frankie. "You promised to be the best person you can be."

"Right, and if I break those promises, I won't be the best person I can be, Frankie," I say.

"Those promises were made by the person you were then. You are a different person now. You have to let yourself think about who you are now, and whether those are still the right promises based on what you know *now*."

"In other words, I might need to change my mind to Be the best person I can now?"

"Yup. When you get watered, you have to let yourself grow. I'm growing from Big to Little."

There are two kinds of change: The kind we choose and the kind that affects us. To paraphrase Shakespeare, some of us achieve change, and others have change thrust upon them.

When Frankie and I were looking at our current choices and thinking about the changes we could make, we were conducting a valuable mental exercise. We were preparing ourselves for the changes we can't control, the ones that are thrust upon us. We were beefing up our resiliency.

William Bridges writes that every transition has three parts: An ending, a neutral period, and a new beginning. "The transition process is really a loop in the life journey, a going out and away from the main flow for a time and then a coming around and back." (*Transitions: Making Sense of Life's Changes*)

Life is dynamic by its nature, and we cannot stop the river of time. The more we resist change, the more painful it will be. When we recognize that life is a roller-coaster, we can enjoy the loops, let ourselves be shaken up, and then get off and embrace the next phase as a joyful new beginning.

> *"I know who I was when I got up this morning,*
> *but I think I must have changed*
> *several times since then."*
>
> LEWIS CARROLL, ALICE IN WONDERLAND

18. Friend

One year, I celebrated Christmas in a boatyard, which is a lonely place to have a holiday. I missed my family; it was just me and my husband, on a sailboat that wasn't floating, and Frankie.

My father always collected lots of presents for me during the year. That year, he mailed a large box of gifts, and I started fussing as soon as the mailman gave it to me. "I live on a *boat*, darn it! Where does he think I'm going to put all this stuff?"

I hauled the box up the ladder onto the boat and opened it. Inside, I found a whole bunch of small gift-wrapped parcels for myself and my husband. We waited until Christmas day, and then we took our time opening them, a few at a time. The most important one wasn't revealed until evening.

It was a lightweight, lumpy package, about six inches high. Inside, I found another white teddy bear, with big black eyes and a bigger, fuzzier nose than Frankie's. The Bear's arms were open wide, just waiting for a hug.

I set the Bear aside, saying, "We don't have room on this boat for any more Bears!"

Frankie watched me from across the boat. He was sitting with a wrapping-paper hat on his head, inhaling egg nog-scented air. He didn't say anything, but I thought I saw him shake his head in dismay.

We all make mistakes. My reaction to the fuzzy white bear was one of them. When I look back, I ask myself, "What were you *thinking?*"

What matters is not the mistake itself, but what happens next. Do we sweep our mistakes under the rug and pretend they didn't happen, so we don't learn anything from them? Do we beat ourselves up with them, saying that they prove we are bad or dumb or unworthy?

Neither of these approaches will make us happier. There's a third way: To find the lesson in each mistake, learn it, and move on with gratitude. Looked at this way, a mistake is a gift. You've just been handed a new tool for your life-toolkit, something to make you wiser and better-equipped for the future.

> *"An error doesn't become a mistake*
> *until you refuse to correct it."*
>
> O.A. BATTISTA

19. Precious

The new white bear sat quietly for a few days. She was nearby when I talked with my father on the phone, and she overheard me say to him, "Thank you for the Christmas gifts, Dad, but I don't have room for any more teddy bears!"

He replied, sounding hurt, "But that one was just so cute! It called out your name, and I couldn't resist. It's just a little bitty thing."

All of a sudden, I heard something different in his words. It was as if he was saying, "When I was shopping, this cute little Bear made me think of you and how much I love you. If you reject the bear, you are rejecting my love."

"Oh," I quickly backpedaled. "I didn't know it was like that. I'm sure I can make room for one more Bear."

When I got off the phone, about ten minutes later, I turned and picked up the small white bear. She didn't hug me like Frankie. She nestled between my cheek and my shoulder.

Then I heard a voice in my ear, and I knew it was hers.

"Hi. I'm Precious. And so are *you*."

I caught my breath in surprise, and she added, "And so is your Dad."

What was missing, when I first saw the fuzzy bear, was gratitude. I had received a gift, but I wasn't grateful for it.

Given the way I usually embrace change, it was surprising that I'd fallen prey to something known as the "negativity bias." That is our mind's natural tendency to perceive something new negatively. In his book on gratitude, *Thanks*, Dr. Robert Emmons says, "…this natural default tendency must be overridden by conscious processes." He goes on to say, "Gratitude is literally one of the few things that can change peoples' lives."

Emmons and others in the field of positive psychology conducted studies that prove long-lasting effects of gratitude, such as lower blood pressure and improved immunity, sleep, and happiness.

Gratitude is something you practice, like mindfulness or Pollyanna's Glad Game. The most common technique is to keep a gratitude journal, which can simply be a notebook on your bedstand. At the end of every day, you write a few things for which you are grateful.

I write three things in my little green notebook each day, and I try not to duplicate them. This year, my list has included such items as time with my nephew, painting technicolor sunflowers, and dental floss. The items on your list will be completely different, but the practice will have the same positive effect.

"If the only prayer you ever say in your entire life is thank you, it will be enough."

MEISTER ECKHART

20. Two-fer

Precious has a completely different personality from either Frank Lloyd Bear or the mischievous Scuppers. She's gentle, shy, and unassuming. Her voice is high-pitched, but soft. She's very feminine.

She is a quiet, caring fountain of love for all beings.

Usually, she and Frankie hang out together. She fits right between his paws, her head snuggled under his chin. I often pick them up and hug them together.

"It's a two-fer," says Frankie. "You get twice as much love from us at the same time."

When I think of a quiet, caring fountain of love for all beings, I think of the Dalai Lama's kindly, compassionate face.

I don't think there's anyone in the world whose smile is better known than his. He just beams! He has said, "My practice, when I see someone, is to smile."

In his article, "Compassion and the Individual," he talks about the importance of smiles, saying, "…a genuine smile really gives us a feeling of freshness and is, I believe, unique to human beings. If these are the smiles we want, then we ourselves must create the reasons for them to appear."

Genuine smiles are definitely the ones I want.

That's why I make it a point to keep Frankie and Precious right in the middle of my life. Often, I make my bed with them sitting on the pillow, but sometimes I set them on my desk when I'm writing. I know they'll make me smile, so they need to be visible, not set off to the side.

I like to create reasons for others to smile, too. The simplest way is to look at another person and think something nice about them. Even if I don't say anything, it's impossible to think something nice and not send them a genuine smile in the process. Usually, they smile back without knowing why.

> *"I smile like a flower, not only with my lips,*
> *but with my whole being."*
>
> RUMI

21. EMERGENCY

Sometimes, when I fly, I take Precious instead of Frankie. She doesn't mind riding in my bag as much as Frankie, who'd rather use his own superpowers to fly.

It was Precious who was traveling with me in Vero Beach, Florida when I received a shocking text message from my dear friend, Philip, in California.

"A terrible thing has happened. My son has died."

I immediately called and spoke with him. He was surrounded by family and friends, but he was in shock. "How can I support you?" I asked, 3000 miles away.

"Just keep sending me your love," he replied.

I was frustrated, because I wanted to do more. I knew that etiquette demanded silly things — I had been on the receiving end of sympathy cards, "in lieu of" charitable donations, houseplants, and floral arrangements. But none of those could touch the pain. Nothing could replace

Tomas, a young man I had once met at his parents' house. I knew he had loved his father a great deal.

My eye fell on Precious, and I knew what to do. Immediately, I started baking cookies.

A few hours later, I took the box containing fragrant fresh-baked cookies and Precious to the post office. The woman behind the counter asked the standard question: "Anything fragile, liquid, perishable, or potentially hazardous in this box?"

At that point, I melted into tears and admitted I was shipping my very own teddy bear to a friend who'd lost his son. The postal employee listened with compassion, and then she said, "Thank you so much."

She went on to tell me about a friend who had recently lost first his daughter, and then his father, to suicide. "I didn't know what to do to support him," said the postal employee. "Now I know. When I get off work, I'm going to get a Bear to send him."

"If it's not your own Bear, you should be sure to charge it up with lots of hugs before sending it, "I recommended. "Here, I'll get you started!"

I leaned across the counter and gave her a big hug, which cheered both of us up immensely and gave the other customers a reason to smile.

It is difficult to know what to do when people around us are suffering. It can make us uncomfortable, so that we want to create distance from them. That's not going to contribute to their well-being, or to our own.

Like gratitude and mindfulness, compassion is a practice. It is something we can develop in ourselves, and when we do, we ease the suffering of others.

Where do you start?

One place to start is by praying, or thinking good thoughts about others. They don't even have to know that you are doing it. I use a simple Loving-Kindness meditation that goes like this:

> May all beings be peaceful.
> May all beings be happy.
> May all beings be safe.
> May all beings awaken to the light of their true nature.
> May all beings be free.

If I have a particular person or group in mind, I replace "all beings" with their name.

Once I've done that, my heart is more attuned to the person who is suffering, and I can figure out what to do next. That might be talking with them, spending some time with them, helping them with a task, or sending them a teddy bear to alleviate their suffering.

> *"Hardship may dishearten at first,*
> *but every hardship passes away.*
> *All despair is followed by hope;*
> *all darkness is followed by sunshine."*

RUMI

22. NETWORK

"You could have sent me on that mission, you know," says Frankie.

"But you weren't with me," I reminded him. "You were on the boat."

"Sometimes, I do my work remotely," he announces. He is climbing into my lap again.

"I have a special hug for you, Margaret," he says.

"Special? Special how?" I ask, intrigued.

"It's from someone who loves you very much."

"Well, you love me very much. You even told me that you love me unconditionally."

"I do," he says, "but somebody else does, too. And that person just sent you a hug through the T.B.N."

Frankie wraps his paws around me and hugs me for quite a long time.

"Wow! That was pretty special." Now I'm curious. "What's this T.B.N?"

"Teddy Bear Network," says Frankie. "That one was from Precious."

"So all those hugs I gave you after Tomas died…?"

"I sent 'em to Precious!" he says, proudly.

"And she delivered them to Philip." Now I understand. When Precious arrived in California, she became a special node in the T.B.N., providing comfort and solace to my friend for several years. In return, she conveyed his affection for me to Frankie.

Then Philip passed away, too, and Precious came back to live with me and Frankie. Sometimes, there's a tiny hint of sadness about her now, because she misses her big, tall California Person. Precious confided in me that Philip was actually part teddy bear, as evidenced by the fuzziness of his white beard. That explains why he was such a good hugger.

Wherever she is and whoever she's with, Precious is completely full of love and compassion for all beings. She is an important member of the Teddy Bear Network, which is connected to all our loved ones, including those who have passed before us.

Do you have photos or artwork on your desk or your refrigerator? That's a common way of staying connected to loved ones. When you display photos or mementos of other people, it provides a reminder and an opportunity to think of them. You can also do it with a background photo on your phone or computer.

If you can, let the person know, because it feels good to know that someone has chosen to display an image of you, or a piece of artwork that you have created. You may find out they have a cherished photo of you.

Sometimes, when I think of someone, I make them a card and put it in the mail. It's a tangible reminder that they are important to me, and I know it will make them feel good to receive it.

If the person is no longer here, like my mother, I can still enjoy a fond memory, and I can direct thoughts of loving-kindness to them, wherever they are. Thich Nhat Hanh wrote, "I know that my mother is always with me. She pretended to die, but that is not true. Our mothers and fathers continue in us."

Across the boundaries of time and space, we are all as connected as our creative imaginations allow. Just the thought of another person connects us to him or her. Who might be thinking of you right now? Who are you thinking of?

> *"Love is from the infinite, and will remain*
> *until eternity. The seeker of love escapes*
> *the chains of birth and death."*
>
> RUMI

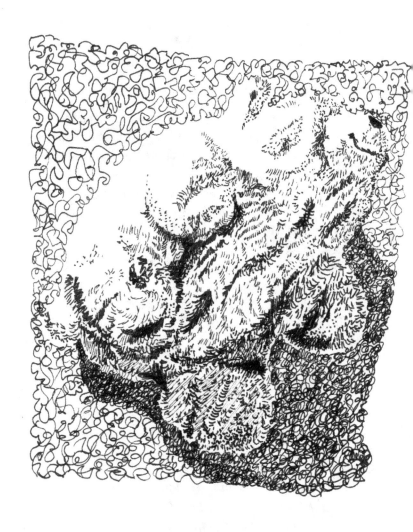

23. NAPS

"That's some heavy stuff," says Frankie. "How are you doing with the writing?"

I heave a deep sigh and look into my empty coffee cup. Frankie may still be enjoying the coffee air, but I need a refill. And maybe a nap.

I haven't said anything out loud about the nap, but Frankie knows what's best. He lures me over to the couch for a snuggle, which turns into a little snooze.

I am awed by his napping abilities. He is a master-napper. Poof! He's asleep. Poof! He's wide awake again, and ready to Be.

He gently corrects me. "Even when I'm napping, I Be. But when I wake up, I can Be and hug and talk, all at the same time."

Sleep is something we all do, but trying to get enough can be pretty stressful. In the United States, 85% of people struggle with sleep, made miserable by insomnia, apnea, or just being too busy to get enough horizontal hours.

If you are one of them, try sleeping with a teddy bear.

A 2010 survey conducted in the U.K. by the Travelodge hotel chain found that about a third of adults sleep with a teddy bear. Psychologist Corrine Sweet commented on the study, "It evokes a sense of peace, security and comfort. It's human nature to crave these feelings from childhood to adult life."

Besides the teddy bear, there are also changes in lifestyle that can help you sleep better. Two practices that were discussed in previous chapters have been scientifically proven to improve the quality of sleep: Meditation and gratitude.

Two others that incorporate movement and meditation have also been proven to improve sleep: Yoga, which was studied at UCLA, and tai chi, which was studied at Harvard. Regarding the participants in the tai chi study, Dr. Michael Irwin said, "They took the least time to fall asleep, had fewer awakenings, and felt better rested. Overall their sleep was better."

"A ruffled mind makes a restless pillow."

CHARLOTTE BRONTË

24. TRAVEL

Frankie has traveled more than most Bears. He's sailed on small boats in the Atlantic and the Pacific and the Gulf of Mexico. He knows all the good anchorages in Puget Sound. He's also driven to all four corners of North America, including British Columbia, San Diego, Key West, and Newfoundland.

He tells me he's at home wherever he is.

"Well, except maybe stuffed into a suitcase," he admits. I know he'd rather do the flying himself, but once in a while, he has to endure the indignity of riding inside my bag.

Once he gets out of the bag and samples the new air, though, he's thoroughly at home, wherever we have landed.

His complacency is completely at odds with my cat, who nearly went insane in a strange motel room. She didn't want space, she wanted security. She was always happier sleeping in the van, a familiar, but tiny, space.

"What do you prefer, Margaret?" asks Frankie.

"I love adventures," I admit, "but if I have to sleep in a strange place…"

"…you want your Bear!" He finishes my sentence triumphantly.

He is confident of his place in my world, no matter where in the world that is.

Right now, we're staying at a friend's house in Bellingham, Washington, and he's curled up on the couch with a new friend, Pola. As in "Pola Bear." She looks like a miniature version of him, the same face, the same posture, but about half his size. Her tag declares her to be a Gund Snuffles, so they are distantly related.

Pola rarely travels, which explains why she looks younger, but is a full eight years older than Frankie.

"Traveling gives you and me character," says Frankie. It's a graceful way to explain his shabbiness and my crows' feet.

Last week, he was with me in California, at another friend's house, where he spent his time looking out the window at deer and wild turkeys. Before that, we were staying in the cozy basement guest-room of relatives in Ohio. Everywhere I go, he goes.

"Where's your favorite place, Frankie?" I ask him.

His round black eyes look surprised at the question. "Right here, Margaret."

I should have known the answer.

I am of two minds about traveling. One is based on Mark Twain's famous statement, "Travel is fatal to prejudice, bigotry and narrow-mindedness, and many of our people need it sorely on these accounts."

The other, however, is based on the words of Ralph Waldo Emerson, who wrote, "At home I dream that at Naples...I can be intoxicated with beauty, and lose my sadness. I pack my trunk, embrace my friends, embark on the sea, and at last wake up in Naples, and there beside me is the stern fact, the sad self, unrelenting, identical, that I fled from."

In other words, wherever you go, there you are.

The problem with travel is that those who do it usually consider themselves superior to those who do not. And those who do not generally feel deprived and envious, despite the fact that their lives can be just as exciting, fascinating, and fulfilling as those who do.

The happy medium is to recognize that either life, mobile or stationary, is completely valid, and neither one is better than the other.

"Our minds travel when our bodies
are forced to stay at home."

RALPH WALDO EMERSON

25. Photos

Yesterday, it was a beautiful day, and I went for a walk along the waterfront with a new friend. Afterwards, we sat in a top-floor café in an old brick building. The sun poured in the windows, and she glowed inside and out. I pulled out my phone to take a picture, and she panicked.

"Oh, no! I hate having my picture taken! I always look terrible." Although the sun was still shining, she turned off her internal glow.

I tried taking the photo anyway, but when I showed it to her, she made me delete it.

This is in contrast to Frankie's reaction to photos. He's the ultimate furry ham.

"Me! Me! Me! I want to be in the picture!"

Every time I take out the camera, he is eager to be included. It's not narcissism; it's something more subtle.

We sit down to talk about it.

"I am who I am," he says.

"What's that got to do with cameras?" I ask.

"Everything, and nothing," he says, maddeningly.

I wait in silence for him to explain. The only sound is the hum of the refrigerator. He hums along as he collects his thoughts.

"When you say, 'Let's take a picture,' you see something good, or at least interesting, in the present moment," he begins.

"…and you are good and interesting?" I ask, hopefully.

"No, that's not it at all. I just am." He tries another approach. "The camera's only a tool. It captures what is."

"You're saying the lens does not judge?"

"Right! The camera loves me unconditionally. It loves you unconditionally, too. When we live in the present moment, we're always good enough to be in the photo."

I used to dread mirrors. Looking at my flaws and imperfections left me feeling depressed and hopeless. Then I did some personal growth work that required me to look into a mirror and really see myself.

At first, it was awful. I hated picking up that mirror! Eventually, I got used to it. Now, when I look into a mirror, I recognize that "I yam what I yam," as Popeye says.

I have learned to be honest about what I see, and to practice self-compassion.

"Compassion isn't some kind of self-improvement project or ideal that we're trying to live up to. Having compassion starts and ends with having compassion for all those unwanted parts of ourselves, all those imperfections that we don't even want to look at," writes Pema Chodron, a Buddhist nun and author. Some of those imperfections are external, and some of them are internal.

Dr. Kristin Neff distinguishes between self-compassion and self-pity or self-indulgence. "Instead of mercilessly judging and criticizing yourself for various inadequacies or shortcomings, self-compassion means you are kind and understanding when confronted with personal failings."

Frankie isn't bothered by the fact that his nose is worn, or his fur is not as white and fluffy as it used to be. He not only has compassion for all beings, he has it for himself, as well.

> *"To love oneself is the beginning*
> *of a life-long romance."*
>
> OSCAR WILDE

26. FEAR

Lately, I've been struggling with something called "anxiety disorder." Frankie tries to comfort me with his wisdom.

"Everything always turns out OK. There's nothing to be afraid of," he says. "Remember that time you left me under the bed in the hotel?"

I remember it well. My husband and I had packed everything in our room, locked the door, and carried our luggage down a couple of flights of steps to the car. We returned the key and got in the car, ready to drive back to Seattle from San Francisco. A half-block away, I noticed that Frankie wasn't riding shotgun between the seats. "OH NO!" I shrieked.

My husband slammed on the brakes, thinking I was referring to something in the chaotic San Francisco traffic.

"We have to go back for Frankie!" I continued, my voice several octaves higher than usual.

We drove around the block, and I went back inside the hotel and explained my dilemma.

"I left something valuable in my room." The clerk's eyebrows were raised in surprise as I added, "My teddy bear."

He hadn't even had time to put the key away; it was sitting where I'd left it on the counter. I pounded up the stairs to our room and unlocked the door, breathless.

Frankie was tangled in the white bedspread, halfway under the bed, fast asleep.

He hadn't even noticed that we had left.

I scooped him up and hugged him tightly. "It was terrible! I was afraid I'd lost you forever!" I told him.

"Well, you didn't," he replied, nonplussed. "I'm right here. And so are you."

I could never convey to Frankie the anxiety and panic of that day. Twenty years later, I say, "I can't believe you didn't even notice that we left without you! That could have changed the course of history!"

Frankie gives a little chuckle. Then he reminds me, "I'm right here. And so are you."

There are hundreds of named phobias, and just reading the lists is an entertaining pastime. Who out there suffers from porphyrophobia, fear of the color purple, or phobophobia, fear of phobias?

My own phobias are pretty garden-variety: Cynophobia, fear of dogs, and ligyrophobia, fear of loud noises. I also suffer from fear-of-losing-your-teddy-bear, although I cannot find a term for that.

The problem with anxiety disorder is that your brain becomes full of irrational fear, which doesn't go away when the teddy bear is found or the source of the loud noise goes away. Even when there is no external threat, the brain and body produce stress hormones, making it difficult to function normally.

One method for treating anxiety is mindfulness therapy. Just like mindfulness meditation, these therapeutic techniques help you focus your attention on the present moment in a non-judgmental way and can help rewire the stress response brought about by anxiety.

"Anxiety is the dizziness of freedom."

SØREN KIERKEGAARD

27. FORT

Anxiety disorder is a funny thing. It's not that I'm afraid of something particular, like a cockroach or an upcoming public speaking engagement. My body just spontaneously goes into flight response and sends all kinds of scared, weird hormones to my brain.

My heart starts pounding, and I get light-headed and shaky. I have learned to deal with it by crawling into bed with Frankie.

For the first time in my life, I pull the covers all the way up over my head.

In the filtered light of the coverlet, I can see Frankie beaming at me. He calms me down, and we take a nap.

One day, my husband came looking for me in the house and couldn't find me. I wasn't under the covers with Frankie, so he checked the closet. You never know where you'll find someone with anxiety disorder.

To his surprise, Frankie and I were on the floor next to the bed, a space less than two feet wide.

"Are you OK?" he asked.

"We're fine," Frankie and I answered in unison.

"What are you doing?" he lingered, curious.

"It's a blanket fort," I explained. "We're very happy here, and we'll come out when we're ready."

Sure enough, when we heard dinner was on the table, we crawled out of our blanket fort. It was the most successful treatment I'd found for anxiety.

From that time on, I told people I had "Blanket Fort Disorder" instead of anxiety. It sounded like so much fun, my friends wanted to come over and join me and Frankie.

"Are you sure you want to put that in the book, Margaret?" asks Frankie.

"Why not?"

"It could get awfully crowded in there. We can't just invite everybody in the world into our blanket fort."

I stare at him incredulously. He gazes back at me, then shakes himself and says, more to himself than to me, "What am I thinking? Of course we can invite everybody in the world into our blanket fort! They might have to bring more blankets, though."

"And more Bears?" I ask.

"Ha!" he chortles. "That's the best part!"

I'm a firm believer in humor therapy for just about everything. I think the best way to get over a cold is to sleep a lot, eat hot-and-sour soup, and watch funny movies. The best way to deal with a boo-boo is to draw smiley-faces on the bandaid. Lots of mood disorders can be improved with a blanket fort.

What makes you laugh? It's different with every person, but one thing is certain: Laughter is contagious. Hearing someone else laugh can make you laugh, even if you don't know what the joke's about. There are even physical practices like laugher yoga, where you put your hands on your belly and make ha-ha noises. Once you get started, natural laughter takes over.

Laughter is proven to boost immunity, trigger endorphins, improve circulation, and decrease pain. There's no reason to hold back: Laughter really *is* the best medicine.

"Do you know what I like about comedy?
You can't laugh and be afraid at the same time."

STEPHEN COLBERT

28. AGING

Every year or so, when he was younger, Frankie used to go into the washing machine. I would specifically look for a front-loading washer, the kind without an agitator, because I didn't think agitation was good for him. I knew it wasn't good for me.

Even then, it was a nerve-wracking process for both of us. What if the wash and rinse cycles were too long, and he ran out of air? What if he had an allergic reaction to the soap, and his fur fell out?

I would sit in front of the washing machine, wringing my hands and reassuring him through the glass. I'm sure I looked like a crazy lady, talking to the washing machine in the Laundromat.

When he came out, always much whiter than he'd gone in, I'd dry him in the sunshine. I always wondered what was inside my furry friend, because he seemed to be losing weight over the years.

Eventually, he became so worn that I was afraid to put him into the washing machine, for fear he'd fall apart completely. I hugged him more and more gingerly.

Frankie's aging process was a lot like a human's. His skin sagged and his fur went from snow-white to dingy gray. Along the way, he gained more perspective and wisdom from his life experiences.

"Frankie, how come you never complain about getting old?" I ask him.

"It wouldn't do any good," he says, shrugging.

"It wouldn't?"

"Nope. Complaining doesn't stop things from happening. It just makes them less fun when they do."

Jimmy Buffett has a great lyric about aging: "Wrinkles only go where the smiles have been." I have lots of wrinkles around my eyes, the radiant kind that look like little sunbeams. I'm proud of my sunbeam-eyes.

Frankie's nose used to be solid brown, with a slightly fuzzy texture. It's now worn in the middle, and the part that's worn looks like a smooth pink heart. He's proud of his heart-nose.

The years each of us has lived leave their marks on our bodies. Working in the garden gives you freckles. Raising children gives you gray hairs. Awesome rock concerts in your twenties make you go "what? what?" in your sixties.

Scars, which are evidence of the most traumatic events to our fragile bodies, provide great stories. Birthdays are an achievement to be celebrated: You have traveled 586 million miles around the sun since the last one.

Every moment makes you more uniquely you.

Enjoy the fascinating process of aging. Getting older may not be comfortable, but it beats the only alternative we have in this world.

"Beautiful young people are accidents of nature,
but beautiful old people are works of art."

ELEANOR ROOSEVELT

29. MIRACLE

One day, I arrange a big surprise. Frankie is going to Suzi's Bear Spa, in Santa Clara, California.

Suzi is a dear friend who calls herself a "dollmaker." I call her a sculptor. She creates fanciful creatures and expressive miniature humans out of three-dimensional mixed media, like fabric and stuffing — the same things that Frankie is made from.

She picks us up in San Jose, and Frankie rides on my lap in the front seat. His gaze takes in the soft hills around Silicon Valley, which have a unique color that I have heard called "Teddy Bear Brown."

When we arrive at Suzi's house, we sit down and start talking about life, relationships, plans, dreams, and family. I am so comfortable, I can talk about anything with Suzi, and so can Frankie.

She puts Frankie in her lap and opens up the seam under his arm. She pulls on his stuffing as we talk, and eventually it all comes out in a single blob.

It's not blob-shaped, though. Frankie's insides are shaped exactly like Frankie's outsides. They're a little lumpier and smaller, without the eyes and nose, but I know without a doubt that's my Bear.

A rush of emotion overwhelms me. I can't believe I am seeing Frankie's outsides and insides separated. He is so real to me, I didn't know this was possible. If you did it to a human…well, that would be messy and they'd never go back together again.

Without the stuffing, Frankie's outsides — his fur and his features — maintain some of their shape, but he looks older and more fragile than ever.

After showing him to me, Suzi puts his outsides into a mesh bag and takes him out to the garage, where the washing machine is.

I worry that he will drown without Air. I worry that I can't talk to him while he's in the washer. But it's only half of him, the outside half. His insides are safe and sound, right in front of me.

After the wash cycle, Suzi puts the outsides into the dryer.

"Are you sure it's OK?" I ask, anxiously. I am terrified that he'll shrink, or disintegrate, or that his fur will curl. She reassures me, smiling at my mother-hen nervousness. She takes me out to the garden to pick fresh kale and tomatoes. Then she sits me down at the kitchen table and distracts me with lunch from the kale and tomatoes.

When Frankie's outsides come back from the dryer, they are bright white and fluffy.

Suzi carefully re-inserts his insides, then begins adding additional stuffing. When she's satisfied, she uses a ladder stitch to sew up the hole under his arm. Then she holds him out to me.

I burst into tears. He is *beautiful.* He's big and white and fluffy, just like he was 21 years earlier. At first, I just stare at him. Then he starts bouncing up and down, full of youthful energy.

"Whee! Whee! Whee!" He flies up to the ceiling and back into my hands.

It's a miracle. Frank Lloyd Bear has been reincarnated in front of my eyes. He stops flying and bursts into a fit of giggles.

"Reincarnated AGAIN?" he says, laughing uncontrollably. "Dang! I was feeling so enlightened! I was sure I was going to reach Nirvana this time."

"There's a very famous book by Jack Kornfield that describes your situation," I tell him.

"What's that," he asks, curiously.

"*After the Ecstasy, the Laundry.*"

I knew a woman, married to a much younger man, who chose to have a facelift. She was tired of looking like her husband's mother. But something went wrong in the surgery; a nerve was damaged, and for the rest of her life, she looked as if she'd had a stroke. Now, when she went out with her husband, she looked like his grandmother.

Such a quick attempt to remake our bodies entails a huge amount of risk. But there are other options, slower ways to change our bodies.

We can exercise, slowly building muscle to hold us upright in our old age. We can change our diets, removing unhealthy foods and replacing them with others that make us feel better. We can laugh more.

Most importantly, we can change our minds. With practice, we can become more mindful and more grateful. We always have the option of replacing old, unhealthy views of ourselves and the world around us with new ones that are healthier and happier.

"You're always free to change your mind and choose a different future, or a different past."

RICHARD BACH

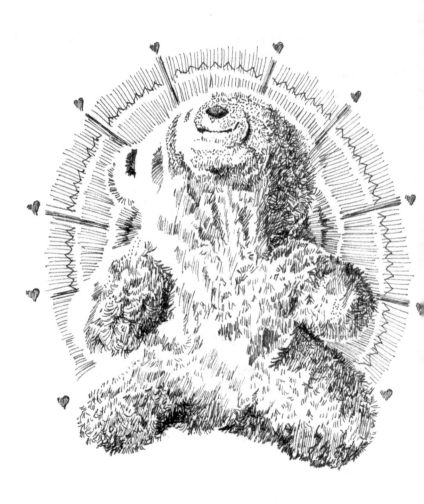

30. REINCARNATION

Frankie's body looks and feels different after his reincarnation, but his personality is very much the same. He seems to be the same Bear he always was.

Yet there's a powerful stillness to him that makes me more aware of my thinking and doing and running around. When I see him, I want to stop and just Be.

"I think you're becoming wiser," I tell him.

"I think you are," he tells me.

I stick my tongue out at him, just to prove that I am not becoming wiser.

"I haven't changed, really," he says. "I'm still who I was yesterday, and the day before, and the day before that, and tomorrow. Even though I'm different."

I'm scratching my head, trying to understand the puzzle that is Bear wisdom.

"Time is an illusion, like a river. It's made of moments, the way a river is made of droplets. Bears live outside Time," he explains.

"You mean you can live forever?"

"I could, but I don't want to," he says. "Not without you."

Is it only Bears who live outside time, or is it possible that we can, as well? Most spiritual practices tell us that we do, whether it is the Sufi belief that we are Divine Light or the Christian concept of Heaven. Some Buddhists believe in Samsara, the wheel of life. This is a repeated cycle that includes birth, life, death and returning to life via birth again.

Each of these belief systems provides us with an explanation for our day-to-day suffering and how it relates to the bigger picture. In doing so, they give us hope.

The other thing that gives us hope is love.

There are a million different views about love, but we all know it when we feel it. And we all feel it, which is why it gives us hope. The fact that we all love means we are all connected in an invisible way.

A few years ago, scientists found the largest organism on earth, a mushroom called the honey fungus. The parts that stuck out of the ground, called the "fruiting bodies," were just the visible part; the actual being was 2.4 miles across.

Perhaps we are just the fruiting bodies of some vast organism, connected beneath the surface and popping up for light and air. If so, living a happier, more joyful life will not only improve the world as it is, but will make it a better one for future generations.

"Enlightenment is intimacy with all things."

DOGEN ZENJI

31. Truth

When I was younger, I didn't love myself at all. I considered myself completely unlovable, a waste of humanity.

"Nobody likes me, everybody hates me, I'm going out and eat worms."

Along came Frank Lloyd Bear. He liked me. He loved me. He was always there for me. He was my enlightened Buddha Bear.

But the hard truth is, Frankie is not alive at all. He's a Gund Snuffles® Bear, Platinum Edition. How can something so simple enhance my life so much?

I've always had an incredibly powerful imagination. I spent years of my life tuned into what I called "The Fantasy Channel," where I overlaid better people and situations on top of the life I was living. Nobody knew; it was all in my head.

One day, I told my friend Carlos about living tuned into the Fantasy Channel all the time. Carlos is a very wise, thoughtful man who happens to be Suzi's life partner.

"I don't think that's very good for you, hmm?" was his comment.

Under his patient gaze, I squirmed. He was right, but I hated to admit it.

I took some time to think about it, and I decided that I agreed with Carlos. I needed to live in the present, to be satisfied with real memories and achievable dreams instead of crazed fantasies of being a completely different person. I took a deep breath, and — click! — I switched off the Fantasy Channel in my head.

Changing the way I thought was a painful process.

I cried with Frankie a lot for the next few months. He talked to me and encouraged me, just as he always has.

Something was different, though. With the Fantasy Channel silent, I began to recognize that Frank Lloyd Bear *was* me. I had given him the best parts of me, to hold until I was ready. He held my wisdom, my unconditional love, my vulnerability, my joy and contentment. He knew who I really was inside: A happy, loving little girl.

That little girl has often been afraid to come out and play, which is why Frankie is so alive. Frankie lives, acts, and speaks for her.

With that realization, Frank Lloyd Bear and I became equals. He no longer carries the wisdom and vulnerability for both of us. Now we share it, along with the joy.

I can see he's just a stuffed bear, and he can see I'm just a squishy human.

Both of us live in the present moment.

Both of us embrace our Big and Little selves.

Both of us love unconditionally.

Both of us like blowing car horns, playing in the snow, and breathing cookie-scented air.

Both of us are willing to embrace change.

Both of us are perfectly imperfect.

Both of us can write a good book.

And both of us are delighted to Be in this world, together.

> *"If you will practice being fictional for a while, you will understand that fictional characters are sometimes more real than people with bodies and heartbeats."*
>
> RICHARD BACH

Resources and Further Reading

Frankie's philosophy grew from an eclectic set of influences. Although a great deal of wisdom comes from sharing a cup of tea with a fellow seeker, it would be impossible for every reader to have a cup of tea and a conversation with Frankie's mentors. As an alternative, here are some written resources and organizations that may assist you along your unique path.

Books

Richard Bach, *Illusions: The Adventures of a Reluctant Messiah*, Dell, 1989.

Richard Bode, *First You Have to Row a Little Boat: Reflections on Life & Living*, Grand Central Publishing, 1995.

William Bridges, *Transitions: Making Sense of Life's Changes*, De Capo Press, 2004.

Thich Nhat Hanh, *Peace Is Every Step: The Path of Mindfulness in Everyday Life*, Bantam, 1992.

Benjamin Hoff, *The Tao of Pooh*, Penguin Books, 1983.

Pir Vilayat Inayat Khan, *Awakening: A Sufi Experience*, Tarcher/Putnam, 1999.

Jack Kornfield, *After the Ecstasy, the Laundry: How the Heart Grows Wise on the Spiritual Path*, Bantam, 2001.

A. A. Milne, *Winnie-the-Pooh*, 1926.

Kristin Neff, *Self-Compassion*, William Morrow, 2010.

Eleanor H. Porter, *Pollyanna*, 1913.

Don Miguel Ruiz, *The Four Agreements*, Amber-Allen Publishing, 1997.

The Essential Rumi, translated by Coleman Barks, HarperCollins, 2004.

Organizations and Websites

Portland Insight Meditation Community: www.portlandinsight.org
My favorite Theravada Buddhist teacher, Robert Beatty, has published many of his teachings on the P.I.M.C. website in text, video, and audio formats. He also leads retreats, mainly in the Pacific Northwest.

The Center for Non-Violent Communication: cnvc.org
You can get a taste of non-violent communication, also known as compassionate communication, by searching for Marshall Rosenberg on YouTube. Then go to the CNVC website to order materials or find a class with a certified trainer near you.

Co-Dependents Anonymous: coda.org
CODA is a 12-step program for people who want to develop more healthy and loving relationships. There are meetings all over the world, and the website contains a wealth of information.

International Taoist Tai Chi Society: taoist.org
Tai Chi is a moving meditation that can be practiced by anyone; it promotes physical, mental and spiritual well-being.

Insight Timer: insighttimer.com
This is an app you can download for your phone that makes it easy to have a daily meditation practice.

Happy Spots: 1meps.com/happyspots
You can read about Happy Spots and download free ones on my website. There are links there to the Happy Spot YouTube video and the Happy Spot Facebook page.

Frankie's favorite recipes: foodiegazette.com/frankie
Frankie loves fresh-baked cookies, spiced cider, and curry. His favorite recipes are available on the Foodie Gazette.

GRATITUDE

I consider myself the luckiest girl in the world, because my Dad, Henry Schulte, is an author who understands the book-writing process. Thank you for being patient with me and your grand-bear.

To David Schulte, who read the manuscript with tough love and made sure it was ready for the world.

To Sharon Stellrecht, who has been known to include homemade cookies when she forwards my mail.

To Barry Stellrecht, Julie Schulte, and Julie Miller, who helped Frankie develop his distinctive voice and his loving message for the world.

To Suzi Mauck, the teddy bear miracle-worker.

To Mr. Silent G, who cooked for me while I sat and drew pictures of teddy bears, and who gave Frankie his first (and only) cigar.

To Roger Cunningham, Philip and Marilyn Lange, and Carlos Puig, who left guiding footsteps for me along the Eightfold Path.

To Karen and Bill Jake, who provided a wheeled writer's cottage known as "The Loaf," and to Jacqui Mac-Connell, who asked me to house-sit during NaNoWriMo. Here's what I wrote at your house!

To Patrick Inman, without whom there would be no Frank Lloyd Bear. When you mailed that box in 1993, you changed the course of history.

If you liked it, please let me know.

Email: frankie@1meps.com

On the web: 1meps.com/frankie

Your friend,

frankie

1993   2003   2016